# Bankruptcy Basics:

*Chapter 7
and Chapter 13*

*To my parents who have always been
very supportive of everything I do.*

Parker Press Inc.
Briarcliff Manor, NY 10510

ISBN: 978-1-941760-22-2

For the latest information and updates to this material, check out:
http://www.reallifelegal.com/updates

# Bankruptcy Basics:
## *Chapter 7 and Chapter 13*

**Marina Ricci, Esq.**

**Real Life Legal**™

*Helpful Guides for Everyday Legal Matters*

Parker Press Inc.

# Contents

# Contents

# What This Book's About

Bankruptcy refers to the legal procedure in the U.S. that enables individuals and businesses to eliminate or repay debts under the protection of the federal bankruptcy court.

Bankruptcy did not exist in ancient times because individuals who could not pay their debts were forced into indentured servitude. For many today, being at the mercy of their creditors is another form of indentured servitude. However in modern times, bankruptcy law enables individuals to get out of debt or to restructure their debt in a way that enables them to pay their creditors. Bankruptcy has also become a way for business to reorganize and keep afloat in hard economic times.

Different countries have different laws concerning bankruptcy. Some countries do not have bankruptcy laws while others only have laws that pertain to businesses. The U.S. has a federal law which helps people who have too much debt.

While the broader economic climate from the mortgage crisis to global economics affects us all, some have been harder hit than others. Debt can accumulate if you're out of work for an extended period of time or incur high medical expenses. Although we hear that economic times are improving, that is not true for everyone.

In 2014, there was an average of 75,000 bankruptcy filings per month. About a million individuals and businesses filed for bankruptcy in the United States.

Filing for bankruptcy may be a good option if you have accumulated debt because you have lost your job, or you face foreclosure on your home or repossession of your car. Bankruptcy can be the best way to get back on your feet and start fresh and debt free. With the help of the bankruptcy process, you may be able to better manage monthly bill payments and decrease the interest rate on those bills or eliminate them altogether.

# Why Bankruptcy?

In the U.S. today, individuals file for bankruptcy because they: (1) can't pay their debt and have very little income or property, or (2) are behind in making payments on their debt and want to keep their property, such as a home or car. Bankruptcy law has become a way for individuals to get out of debt or to restructure their debt in a way that enables them to pay their creditors. Other forms of bankruptcy filings can also help a business reorganize and keep afloat in tough economic times.

Bankruptcy laws may seem complicated at first, but they can be broken down into manageable pieces. The goal here is for you to understand whether or not it makes sense for you to file for bankruptcy, and what to expect if you go forward. Filing for bankruptcy is a big step and if you're thinking about filing, care should be taken to make sure you will not be worse off by filing.

In the U.S. today, most people file for bankruptcy because they're not able to pay their debts and have very little income or property, or because they're behind in their payments and want to keep their homes or cars.

While bankruptcy is a way to eliminate all or partial debt, it is also a way for creditors to have access to your property. As a result, many factors should be considered before any action is taken when it comes to bankruptcy. Much thought goes into the decision as to whether a bankruptcy filing is right for you.

---

*There are two basic types of bankruptcies: Chapter 7 refers to liquidation of assets and elimination of most debt, and Chapter 13 aims to reorganize debts so that payments continue at a manageable level.*

---

## Should I Hire an Attorney for a Bankruptcy Filing?

After extensive changes to the bankruptcy laws in 2005, it's tougher for individuals to file for bankruptcy without an attorney. The process today has far more requirements and documents which is why we recommend you hire an experienced bankruptcy attorney to help you. With or without an attorney, it is very important to understand how to do it properly and how it will impact your future.

*A qualified attorney with experience in bankruptcy filings is the best person to counsel you on what makes sense in your situation.*

Filing the proper paperwork that is correctly prepared is essential to having a successful outcome. The detailed requirements must be met and often an experienced bankruptcy attorney knows the ropes and the lingo to make things go more smoothly.

# Bankruptcy Fundamentals

Several types of bankruptcy filings are permitted under federal law. This book covers two types of bankruptcies used by individuals, known as Chapter 7 and Chapter 13.

Chapter 7 bankruptcy is generally filed by individuals who have little or no income or income that falls under the median allowed for their household size. Typically after expenses are paid, there is no other disposable income for someone who files a Chapter 7 bankruptcy.

- You can file for Chapter 7 bankruptcy every eight years and it is used to eliminate debt and to stop a **"garnishment."** A garnishment is a court-ordered payment from your wages to pay debt.

- The length of a Chapter 7 bankruptcy is about four months from the time of filing.

- Once a case is filed, it takes about 4-6 weeks in order to receive a hearing date and then about sixty days to receive a **"discharge"** of all debts.

Chapter 13 bankruptcy is a repayment plan rather than a full bankruptcy that eliminates debt. Most individuals have to pay at least ten percent of their **"unsecured debt."** This type of bankruptcy is filed by those individuals whose income exceeds the maximum **"median income"** allowed for their household size, are behind in home or car payments, or who have filed a Chapter 7 within the last eight years.

Often people who have filed for Chapter 7 bankruptcy within the last eight years will file a Chapter 13 bankruptcy in order to stop an action from taking place, such as a pending garnishment. A Chapter 13 bankruptcy can last anywhere between thirty-six to sixty months, and sometimes shorter depending on the type of debt and the amount being paid off every month.

## Types of Federal Bankruptcies:

- Chapter 7: Eliminates debt.
- Chapter 9: Used by government entities.
- Chapter 11: For large businesses to restructure debt.
- Chapter 12: For people who have mostly farm income.
- Chapter 13: Used to restructure and repay debt.

This book will discuss bankruptcies under Chapters 7 and 13.

# Chapter 7 Bankruptcy

Chapter 7 bankruptcies are filed by people who seek to eliminate the maximum amount of debt possible. With a Chapter 7 bankruptcy, a court will liquidate (i.e., sell) most of your property to pay down your debt. Only assets not pledged as collateral for a loan can be sold. For example, a home subject to a mortgage or a car subject to a **"lien"** could not be sold to pay other creditors.

Once the available assets are sold or used to pay down debt, any remaining debt (such as credit card debt or medical bills) can be discharged, meaning you will no longer be liable to pay it.

With this type of bankruptcy, you are allowed to keep some of your property if it is covered by an exemption. Most people who file for bankruptcy under Chapter 7 own few assets other than assets that are exempt. Property **"exemptions"** are discussed on pages 57–58.

A person (or married couple) can be eligible to file for bankruptcy depending on household size, median income in the state of residence and value of assets. All of these factors are taken into account to determine if you're eligible to file.

---

*People who file Chapter 7 bankruptcy have low or no income and have little property. Their debt far exceeds their ability to pay it back.*

---

In 2014, over three-fourths of the bankruptcies filed in the United States were Chapter 7 bankruptcies.

As part of a Chapter 7 filing, you must attend what's known as a **"341 hearing"**. At this hearing it is determined whether you qualify for a Chapter 7 filing, based on the amount of money or property you have. Sometimes you have more assets than can be protected.

If you qualify at the 341 hearing and all the paperwork is filed properly, you will receive a discharge, which means all the debt that could be eliminated under the bankruptcy is eliminated.

## Basics on Chapter 7 Bankruptcy

Chapter 7 aims to liquidate assets to pay down debt.

- It's used to eliminate debt and stop garnishments. The process takes about four months from the time of filing to the end of the case.

- You must attend a hearing about your property.

# Chapter 13 Bankruptcy

Chapter 13 bankruptcy doesn't aim to eliminate your debt, but creates a payment plan so you can affordably pay back all or a percentage of your creditors over a period of thirty-six to sixty months. With this type of bankruptcy, a person has to be able to show that he or she has sufficient income to pay back debt.

Chapter 13 is generally filed by those who make too much money for a Chapter 7 filing, or own a lot of equity in their property. If individuals have a lot of property, such as a bank account with considerable money in it, the bankruptcy court can force them to cash out or sell the property in order to pay their creditors.

In 2014, almost one-third of the bankruptcies filed were Chapter 13 bankruptcies. This type of bankruptcy is also filed by people who are behind on house or car payments, and who have already filed a Chapter 7 within the previous eight years.

Many times, an individual who has filed a Chapter 7 bankruptcy within the last eight years will file a Chapter 13 bankruptcy in order to stop an action from taking place, such as a pending garnishment.

## REAL LIFE EXAMPLE

Andy is single and unemployed and has only $1,000 in his bank account. He rents an apartment and all of his property including his car, furniture and appliances are worth $1,000. Andy has total assets of $2,000.

Cheryl is single and works as a desk clerk and makes $60,000 a year. She owns her home and has $20,000 in her savings account. Cheryl has three children who live at home and is having a hard time keeping up with all of her expenses.

Andy would file for Chapter 7 bankruptcy because he has no income and has very few assets in his name. Cheryl, on the other hand, would file a Chapter 13 bankruptcy. She likely has too much income and money in her bank account to qualify for Chapter 7.

If Cheryl's goal is to preserve the equity in what she owns and make a workable plan to repay her debts, Chapter 13 is a good choice. But if not, she may qualify for a Chapter 7 bankruptcy depending on the state where she lives and how it treats her children and her specific monthly expenses.

## Basics on Chapter 13 Bankruptcy

A Chapter 13 bankruptcy is often filed to keep assets and formulate a payment plan to:

- Prevent a home foreclosure sale date.
- Stop a car repossession.
- Pay the IRS.
- Stop a garnishment.

# Not All Debts Are Eliminated in Bankruptcy

Regardless of whether you file a Chapter 7 or a Chapter 13 bankruptcy, not all debts are necessarily eliminated. For example, child support, alimony, certain taxes and government fines are not dischargeable. Any debt that is incurred as a result of fraud (and is proven by the creditor to be fraud) also cannot be eliminated.

In almost all Chapter 13 bankruptcies, past-due support obligations or past-due recent taxes have to be paid fully in order for a plan to be approved.

Any debt that is incurred as a result of fraud (and is proven by the creditor to be fraud) also can't be eliminated. Recent debt (incurred within ninety days of filing) may also have to be paid back in full. Otherwise, a **"debtor"** could go on a shopping spree and rack up credit card debt one week and then file for bankruptcy the next. Here *debtor* refers to a person filing for bankruptcy, but in other contexts it refers to someone who owes money to repay a debt.

# How Often Can You File?

The U.S. bankruptcy laws have timeframes which spell out how long you must wait to file for bankruptcy again, if you've already filed and it has gone through. For people who have credit and debt problems or experience a job loss or high health bills, it's not uncommon to file for either or both types of bankruptcy.

There are limits to how often you can file based on whether you've filed for bankruptcy before, and if so, when that filing was made. Here's how the time frames work:

- If you file a Chapter 7 bankruptcy, you can't file another Chapter 7 bankruptcy for eight years.

- If you file a Chapter 7 bankruptcy, you can file a Chapter 13 bankruptcy after four years and obtain a discharge.

- If you file a Chapter 13 bankruptcy, you generally have to wait six years to file a Chapter 7 bankruptcy.

- If a Chapter 13 bankruptcy is filed, you can file for Chapter 13 bankruptcy again after two years.

## Debts Not Discharged in Bankruptcy

Typically the following debts can't be eliminated with either a Chapter 7 or a Chapter 13 bankruptcy:

- Past-due child support and alimony.
- Tax debts within three years.
- Government fines.
- Debt due to fraud.
- Student loans.
- Debt agreed to in a divorce decree.

## What If Your Bankruptcy Filing Is Dismissed?

If a bankruptcy is dismissed, it means the court did not approve the bankruptcy. The filing rules concerning how often you can file do not apply if the bankruptcy did not go through. They only apply based on the date of the last successful bankruptcy filing.

*Dismissed charges are different from having debts "discharged." If a bankruptcy goes through, debts may be discharged. If a case is dismissed, the case does not go through and no debts are discharged.*

**REAL LIFE EXAMPLE**

John filed for Chapter 7 bankruptcy to get rid of his debt on January 13, 2010. On January 16, 2014, John lost his job and started accumulating a lot of debt. On March 16, 2014, John was hired at a retail store but he earns far less than before and must file for bankruptcy to avoid creditors from suing him for non-payment.

John can likely file a Chapter 13 bankruptcy, since it has been more than four years since his first Chapter 7 bankruptcy filing. However, he will have to wait until January 13, 2018 in order to file another Chapter 7 bankruptcy. An attorney can advise John if it is feasible for him to file Chapter 13 now or wait until 2018 to file Chapter 7.

## State Law Bankruptcy

Chapter 7 and Chapter 13 refer to types of bankruptcy filings under federal law, which are under the jurisdiction of the U.S. Bankruptcy Court. Bankruptcy is filed in a federal court in the state in which you reside. Although federal bankruptcy law applies, each state sets its own rules concerning exemptions, or they can use the federal exemptions.

There may also be additional types of bankruptcy filings authorized under state laws, but they are not covered in this guide. You should check your state's website to learn whether there is a state law bankruptcy filing alternative where you live.

# Credit Counseling

Every debtor has to do a credit counseling class prior to filing for bankruptcy and before the case is finalized. There are specific agencies that give these classes and then issue the specific certificates that have to be filed with the court. You can learn more at: http://www.justice.gov/ust/eo/bapcpa/ccde/index.htm

For a Chapter 7 bankruptcy, the **"debtor education class"** certificate has to be filed within sixty days after the 341 hearing. The 341 hearing generally occurs four to six weeks after a bankruptcy petition is filed. A debtor education class is a mandatory class that must be taken for a bankruptcy to go through.

- If the certificate is not filed on time, the case will close without a discharge, meaning that the bankruptcy will have no effect in eliminating the debt and the creditors would still be able to collect on the debt by suing the debtor.

- If a certificate is not filed, the case can be reopened in order to file the certificate even if the class is completed only after the case is closed.

For a Chapter 13 bankruptcy, the certificate of completion for the debtor education class has to be filed before the case is discharged. A debtor has five years to take the class but it's a good idea to get it done early so that the debtor doesn't forget to do the class altogether.

# Eligibility to File for Bankruptcy

Generally, single or married people who are legal residents of the United States can file for bankruptcy in any state in the United States in which they are residents.

Each form of bankruptcy filing has its own requirements. Typically you must meet income requirements, as well as residency requirements to file for bankruptcy in a federal court, within your state.

While most people file for bankruptcy as individuals, couples who are legally married to each other can file bankruptcy together. Children and parents, siblings, and friends cannot file bankruptcy together although they are able to file individual bankruptcies.

## Chapter 7 Eligibility

To file for Chapter 7 bankruptcy, an individual has to qualify based on income, debt, household size, and the value of the property he or she owns.

- **Household size:** Individuals need to have under the median income for the state in which they live. For example, to qualify for Chapter 7 bankruptcy in Arizona in 2014, a family of four can't have more than $65,550 of pre-tax income. If income exceeds this level, they may be able to file for Chapter 13 bankruptcy.

- **Residency:** Most states determine residence based on where a person has lived for at least ninety-one of the prior 180 days. You apply that state's median income to determine whether they can file.

Median incomes are calculated in gross which means these are before taxes and they are based on family size. They are updated annually and often if there is an option (for people who have lived in more than one state), you select the state where your income falls below the mandated median income. The following link will help you find the state medians for 2014: http://www.justice.gov/ust/eo/bapcpa/meanstesting.htm

Even if your income does not fall below the state's median income, there may still be ways to file Chapter 7 bankruptcy if the income is close to or fairly close to the stated median. For example, if a debtor just lost his job and previously made a lot of money, he would not qualify based on the **"means test."** But since he will make no money going forward, he will qualify overall.

## Chapter 13 Eligibility

A Chapter 13 bankruptcy is a repayment plan for people who may make more than the allowable income or have too much property for a Chapter 7 bankruptcy. With a Chapter 13 bankruptcy, the court works with a debtor to create a plan for the repayment of creditors up to a certain percentage of what they owe.

To be eligible to file a Chapter 13 bankruptcy you must have enough income to cover all your expenses and to make an additional payment representing the amount agreed to settle the debt. These amounts are paid to the bankruptcy court each month. People who fall behind in payments on their home or cars may choose to file for Chapter 13 bankruptcy to avoid losing these assets.

---

*Bankruptcy can be used to avoid having a bank repossess a car or a home. It forces creditors to work together to forge a workable repayment plan.*

---

Even if it seems like there isn't enough money to cover expenses, if an individual can find the money somehow by decreasing expenses to make payments every month for sixty months, then a Chapter 13 bankruptcy can be filed and it will be approved if the paperwork is done correctly.

# Why Choose Filing Chapter 13 over Chapter 7?

You may choose to file for Chapter 13 bankruptcy because you don't qualify under Chapter 7. This can happen if your income exceeds the median income in your state, or your equity in your property is high or your property is worth more than is permitted with the exemptions in your state. Another reason someone may want to file for Chapter 13 is to pay off tax debt or stop a foreclosure. A Chapter 13 filing assists in all of these matters.

---

*Sometimes a person will be eligible to qualify for both a Chapter 7 and a Chapter 13 filing. These determinations depend on the facts in your situation.*

---

Some people are forced to file a Chapter 13 bankruptcy because they are being sued or are about to have wages garnished and they have already filed under Chapter 7 within the last eight years. With few options, the prospect of Chapter 13 payments may be preferable to a garnishment.

It's essential to have a steady source of income when filing a Chapter 13 bankruptcy because the bankruptcy court will not approve the bankruptcy unless you can show you can make the payments over a repayment plan period of thirty-six to sixty months.

Mandy and Victor, married, live in Illinois and they have two kids and are thinking of filing for Chapter 7 bankruptcy. They have an annual gross income of $80,000. They don't have a lot of property together and they have never filed a Chapter 7 before.

Tanya and Harry, married, also live in Illinois and they have no children. They have an annual gross income of $90,000 and they don't have a lot of property.

In this situation, Mandy and Victor will most likely be able to file Chapter 7 bankruptcy because the median income in Illinois for a family of four is around $80,000 gross for 2014. However, Tanya and Harry make more than the allowable income to file a Chapter 7 for a family of two because the permitted gross income for a family of two is around $60,000 and they earn $90,000 gross a year. Tanya and Harry will most likely have to file for Chapter 13 bankruptcy.

# Income Limits

People who file for bankruptcy have to prove to the court that they either (1) don't make more than the required income for a Chapter 7 bankruptcy, or (2) that they have enough steady income to file a Chapter 13 bankruptcy. This proof is calculated in a test called the means test, which is more fully explained by clicking on the following link: http://www.justice.gov/ust/eo/bapcpa/meanstesting.htm

A means test calculation has to be filed with every bankruptcy case in order to show the court whether or not an individual is eligible to file either a Chapter 7 or a Chapter 13 bankruptcy. It is a summary of the previous six months of pre-tax household income.

## Income Limits for Chapter 7

The gross income of a filer must be under the median required for the state and family size. Even if an income level doesn't pass at first, there are many deductions that can be taken that may enable a person to be eligible to file a Chapter 7 bankruptcy. The income limits for Chapter 7 change yearly and they can be found here: http://www.justice.gov/ust/eo/bapcpa/20141101/bci_data/median_income_table.htm

For example, if someone pays a high mortgage or costly medical insurance, this could help a filer pass the means test. In addition, if non-filing spouses are involved and they have their own expenses, this can be beneficial.

---

*Sometimes, the expenses used in the means test or the marital adjustment are critical to enabling a person to file for bankruptcy.*

---

## Income Limits for Chapter 13

In a Chapter 13 bankruptcy filing, the means test is used to determine how much debt the individual has to pay back. Every means test deduction that can be used should be used to keep the payments as low as possible.

If a married person is filing as an individual, and the debt is only in one name, a marital adjustment can be made on the means test to enable an individual to file under Chapter 7, or to lower the amount that has to be paid back on a Chapter 13. The marital adjustment takes into account expenses of the non-filing spouse such as their own bills, car payments, medical expenses, etc.

## REAL LIFE EXAMPLE

Jonathan and Heather want to file for Chapter 7 bankruptcy. Jonathan makes $40,000 gross a year and Heather earns $20,000 gross a year. They live in Florida, have no children and do not own a home. The couple earns too much to file for Chapter 7 bankruptcy in Florida because the median income in that state is roughly $52,000.

However, if Jonathan files for Chapter 7 bankruptcy alone, Heather can put the amount she pays for her bills every month into the marital adjustment in order to qualify Jonathan to file for Chapter 7 bankruptcy under the means test. If the amount she pays per month for her credit card bills is high enough, Jonathan will be able to file for Chapter 7 bankruptcy.

# How a Bankruptcy Proceeding Works

**Bankruptcy is a court proceeding and it is started when a petition and appropriate schedules are filed.**

A bankruptcy proceeding is filed in the federal bankruptcy court located in the county where the debtor lives. Certain elements must be proved from the face of the filing for the application to be considered.

## Creditors Are Represented by Trustees

When a bankruptcy petition is filed, the court appoints trustees to represent the creditors. There are two types of trustees in the bankruptcy court:

A U.S. trustee oversees all filings and their accurateness and also watches for fraud.

An interim trustee is appointed to represent the creditors. This trustee:

- finds property that the debtor owns that is not fully exempted, which can be sold to pay creditors, and
- earns a fee based on the value of property they find and sell.

Trustees can ask for values in writing from experts and can have their own experts value the property.

---

*Bankruptcy trustee fees are based on non-exempt property which is discovered and becomes part of the bankruptcy estate. An attorney can make sure that a debtor maximizes available bankruptcy exemptions which also reduce the trustee fees.*

---

# 341 Hearings

Within four to six weeks after a petition for bankruptcy is filed, a 341 hearing is held. The purpose of the hearing is to determine whether the debtor has assets which can be distributed to creditors.

- The hearing is mandatory and the bankruptcy will not go through to discharge if the hearing is not attended by all debtors who filed. If there is a medical reason why a debtor cannot attend, the trustee and the court have discretion to excuse the hearing.

- The trustee is usually appointed to conduct the hearing and to request additional information from the debtors after a hearing.

To get an idea of how an exemption works, consider this example. Let's say a debtor owns a house he values at $100,000, which is subject to a $50,000 lien.

- The house is eligible for a $15,000 exemption.

- If it turns out the house is really worth $200,000, not $100,000, then the trustees may try to seize the house in order to sell it and pay off creditors.

- The trustees and creditors do not have access to amounts claimed as exemptions. In this example, if the house is really worth $100,000, only $35,000 is available to creditors. (The $50,000 lien and $15,000 exemption combine to keep $65,000 of the house's value unavailable to creditors.)

It's essential to understand the value of your assets and how to maximize exemptions before you do a filing. Otherwise you may be giving up value and worse off economically.

*Exempt items are not touched by the bankruptcy court. Non-exempt items can be seized by the trustee and turned over to creditors. It's essential to carefully assess exemptions before a bankruptcy is filed to avoid huge losses.*

## Providing Necessary Documentation: 521 Docs

Debtors who file for bankruptcy must provide so-called **"521 documents"** to the trustee assigned to their case. These documents include sixty days' worth of proof of income, for the sixty days prior to filing. This typically includes pay stubs and the prior year's tax return, or return last filed.

If the information is not provided promptly after filing, the trustee can decide not to hear the case. If a 341 hearing is not held, the bankruptcy will be dismissed. If an individual did not file taxes in the last year or if he is not required to file taxes, he can sign an affidavit that is notarized saying that he has not filed taxes.

# Bankruptcy Motions: Unfreezing Bank Accounts

In bankruptcy there are many types of motions which the court can request after a bankruptcy is filed. Among the most common are those used to either unfreeze a bank account or to reopen a case after a discharge is filed because no debtor education class certificate has been filed.

Each motion must be accompanied by what's called a **"Notice of Filing."** This notice alerts all parties to activities and motions in your case. Typically an attorney handles motions to make sure they are properly filed and achieve the desired result.

## Creditor Objections

Creditors file what's known as an **"objection"** if they do not agree with a bankruptcy filing. Usually, there are few objections filed in a Chapter 7 bankruptcy. However, if fraud is involved, an objection is possible.

Fraud includes charging up a credit card right before a bankruptcy filing or trying to put a debt into a bankruptcy that is owed to a spouse through a divorce decree. Fraud can also be involved if a filer fails to notify a creditor of the bankruptcy proceeding and the creditor should be notified. An ex-spouse may also raise objections depending on the facts.

Typically these types of objections are resolved by agreeing to pay the creditor or the ex-spouse the money they are owed.

# Automatic Stay: Creditors Cannot Contact or Garnish

An **"automatic stay"** goes into effect the instant a bankruptcy is filed. It stops notified creditors from contacting the debtor or from trying to collect on any debts while the bankruptcy is filed. Once the bankruptcy is done, all active garnishments must be stopped.

In a Chapter 7 bankruptcy, this protection remains in effect for at least four months.

- A creditor may ask for protection to be removed in this time.

- No protection may exist if the debtor has filed another bankruptcy very recently. Even then, however, the debtor is usually still protected since a Chapter 7 bankruptcy only lasts about four months from the start of filing and a creditor has very little time to act.

- This protection can be lifted or removed if a debtor doesn't pay on secured items such as real property and vehicles. This requires a creditor to go to court and pay a fee to repossess the property.

Usually the protection can only be removed after the first bankruptcy hearing, to allow the court to assess whether it wants any of the debtor's property.

If a stay is lifted in a Chapter 7 bankruptcy, the creditor can regain possession of the property. The automatic stay will usually not stop most family law or criminal law proceedings.

# Debt Discharged in Bankruptcy

The debt in a bankruptcy is officially eliminated when the bankruptcy is over and the debtor receives a document called a discharge from the court. A discharge is received sixty days after a 341 bankruptcy hearing which is usually the only hearing required in a Chapter 7 bankruptcy.

Once the discharge is received, a debtor cannot be contacted by the creditor if the creditor was listed in the bankruptcy filing. In some jurisdictions, even if the creditor was not listed in the bankruptcy filing, unless it was done on purpose to commit fraud (e.g., the debtor hid assets known only to certain creditors), the debt is considered part of the bankruptcy filing if it was incurred before the bankruptcy was filed.

*The discharge does not eliminate debt that cannot be eliminated in bankruptcy such as student loans, government fines, or any debt incurred as a result of fraud.*

# Owning Too Much: Asset Cases

When an individual has more property than can be protected in a Chapter 7 bankruptcy, then this is called an **"asset case."** This means that the interim trustee can distribute these excess assets to creditors. This is rare in real life because debtors typically have little or no property and the property they do have is usually not worth anything after exemptions are taken into account.

It is very important to know the value of items when filing a bankruptcy because debtors can lose a lot of money and property if bankruptcies are filed improperly.

## Buying Back Your Property

Let's say you have assets or unprotected equity and you file for bankruptcy. With a buyout, the debtor can offer to pay the trustee the difference between what the property is worth and the amount of the property that is protected by exemptions. The debtor can buy the unprotected part of the property from the trustee without having the trustee sell the property in order to obtain those funds.

### REAL LIFE EXAMPLE

David has a car worth $15,000, which he owns outright. A $5,000 exemption protects the vehicle, but $10,000 in equity is not exempt. The trustee has the right to sell the vehicle to disburse the unprotected $10,000 to David's creditors. Instead, David can bargain with the Trustee and offer, e.g., $7,000 to pay for the car over a six–to-twelve-month period to avoid the sale of the car by the trustee.

The trustee has the option to accept or reject this offer.

- If the trustee sells the car, it would have to remit the first $5,000 in sales proceeds (the exempt amount) to David.

- This factors into the price he may accept from David for David's equity.

- If the trustee tries to sell the car and gets $10,000 for it, he first has to give $5,000 to David, leaving only $5,000 for creditors.

- It makes more sense for the trustee to let David buy the equity in the car for $7,000.

## Reinstating Home and Auto Loans

When a debtor files bankruptcy, any contracts made before the filing that obligate the debtor to pay any amount of money are wiped out. This includes mortgages and car loans, as well as credit card agreements. If a debtor wants to keep the property and continues to pay on it, a special arrangement must be made, known as a **"reaffirmation agreement."**

Reaffirmation agreements will only be approved by the court if they are for necessities. For example, the debtor needs the car to go to work or lives in the home. If a debtor does not sign a reaffirmation agreement, he will not receive credit for making such payments on his credit report because the lender cannot report payments made once a bankruptcy is filed. Thus, a debtor's credit report score cannot be improved by payments made on debt that was not reaffirmed.

After a bankruptcy filing, lenders will send out reaffirmation agreements which permit a pre-bankruptcy lender and debtor to reach an agreement while there is an active bankruptcy.

- This cannot be done once the bankruptcy is discharged.

- If a debt is not reaffirmed, it means that the debtor can walk away from the property at any time without owing anything on the property such as a house or a car.

- When filing bankruptcy, debtors have to make sure that there are only a reasonable number of houses and vehicles for the family size or the court may not allow the reaffirmation to go through if debtors wish to reaffirm.

- Sometimes, if debtors' expenses exceed their income, a judge may schedule a hearing to make sure that they understand what a reaffirmation agreement actually means.

Once property is reaffirmed, a debtor cannot return that property to the lender without consequences, because it's a new binding contract.

## REAL LIFE EXAMPLE

Katie buys a house and takes out a $200,000 mortgage. She files for Chapter 7 bankruptcy a few years later. During the bankruptcy, Katie signs a reaffirmation agreement for the mortgage. After the bankruptcy, Katie's house goes into foreclosure and the mortgage company sues Katie for the amount she still owes after the home is sold in a foreclosure sale.

The mortgage company can sue Katie because she signed a reaffirmation agreement for the mortgage debt. If Katie had not signed the reaffirmation agreement, the mortgage company could still foreclose on Katie's house because it is secured by the mortgage loan but they could not sue Katie for the amount still owed, because the mortgage would have been included in the bankruptcy. Most creditors will allow a debtor to keep and pay on a property that is not reaffirmed, however, some creditors will repossess or foreclose on a property if a reaffirmation is not signed.

---

*Prior to signing any agreements during a bankruptcy, contact a lawyer to prevent from being personally sued and liable for any debts.*

---

# Non-filing Spouses

It is possible to be married and only file a bankruptcy individually. However, when this happens, only the debt of the individual filing will be eliminated.

- If there is joint debt, the spouse not in bankruptcy will still be liable to pay off the full debt, and not just 50% of it. **"Cosigners"** and joint debtors are typically liable for the full debt.

- Household income will be disclosed on both the means test and Schedule I. If the spouses are separated and live in separate households, then income for the non-filing spouse need not be disclosed.

- The non-filing spouse's social security number and name should not be on the petition or anywhere in the filing.

# Converting from a Chapter 7 Bankruptcy to a Chapter 13 Bankruptcy and Vice Versa

In bankruptcy, an individual can convert from Chapter 7 to a Chapter 13 and from a Chapter 13 to a Chapter 7 under the right circumstances.

## Chapter 13 Converting to Chapter 7

A conversion from a Chapter 13 to a Chapter 7 occurs when income goes down or expenses go up and the individual qualifies to file under Chapter 7. To convert:

- A new means test that verifies the current situation must be completed and submitted with a Notice of Filing to let the court know that the individual is converting.

- Amended schedules must be filed to inform the court about the changes that occurred to enable the conversion. Usually a new Schedule I or J and maybe Schedule B are filed. Also a Debtor's Statement of Intention, not required in Chapter 13, must be filed.

---

*Whenever an amendment is made to any bankruptcy schedules, a Notice of Filing has to be filed with a certificate on it saying when the amendment was made and who was given notice.*

---

## Chapter 7 Converting to Chapter 13

A conversion from Chapter 7 to Chapter 13 typically occurs when the trustee finds property or the debtor's income goes up substantially in a very short period of time. A motion must be made to the court to allow such a conversion; the court has to approve a repayment plan (more on that in chapter 6).

A unique situation occurs when an individual converts from a Chapter 13 to a Chapter 7 which allows the debtor to put any debt that was incurred after the Chapter 13 was filed but before the case was converted to be put into the Chapter 7 bankruptcy. In this case, Schedule F has to be amended and a Notice of Filing has to be filed to let the court know that the amendment was made. Because people can be in a Chapter 13 bankruptcy for years before conversion, this becomes a great advantage when medical bills become an issue post-filing.

Phil files for Chapter 13 bankruptcy and two years later gets into a car accident and incurs a lot of medical bills. If he converts his bankruptcy to a Chapter 7 after the accident, all the bills incurred after the Chapter 13 filing can be part of the Chapter 7 bankruptcy and will be discharged.

# Post-discharge Creditor Issues

Creditors can be sanctioned by the court for contacting the debtor after discharge. A debtor should contact an attorney if this happens in order to take proper action, especially if the creditor continues to contact the debtor.

Creditors not given notice of the bankruptcy may still be bound unless they were not notified on account of fraud. Most debts incurred before the bankruptcy filing, are discharged even if they are not listed in a Chapter 7 bankruptcy filing. This is unique to Chapter 7 and does not apply to Chapter 13. In Chapter 13, the creditor must be listed to be bound by the discharge order.

# Waiver of Bankruptcy Filing Fee

Most people filing for bankruptcy have to pay the filing fee to the bankruptcy court. The fee can be waived if the applicant lacks funds and successfully files a **"Forma Pauperis Motion."** With this request, the court looks at the filer's income and expenses. If the judge determines the debtor is living below the poverty level, and Schedules I and J do not show excess funds, the motion may be granted.

Bankruptcy fee waivers are not generally granted in Chapter 13 cases because debtors must show they have funds available to make repayment payments. Often that does not align with a motion that there are insufficient funds to pay the fee, but it can still be attempted.

# Finding Your Case Online via Pacer

Pacer is an online subscription service that is used to access debtor filing information. It includes all information concerning date, filing location and documents in a particular case. Usually a debtor's attorney, and not the debtor, has access to the system.

Attorneys can also use the ECF electronic filing system to both file a bankruptcy petition and motions.

---

*Debtors who do their own filing, pro se (without an attorney), typically file their paperwork in person with the federal bankruptcy clerk in their jurisdiction, using the appropriate forms.*

---

Bankruptcy court locations can be accessed at: http://www.uscourts.gov/Court_Locator.aspx.

The Pacer system can track all filed paperwork from the **"Credit Counseling Certificate"** to the means test.

Once a Chapter 7 bankruptcy is filed, all the property of the individual becomes the property of the bankruptcy court until the case is discharged and closed. This means that if there is property that is found to have value that exemptions cannot protect, that property can be sold by the trustee. In cases such as these, either a buyout is done or the case is converted to a Chapter 13 bankruptcy. A Chapter 7 bankruptcy cannot be voluntarily dismissed by a debtor.

# Forms Required with a Chapter 7 Bankruptcy Filing

**A bankruptcy petition along with specific schedules must be submitted to the U.S. Bankruptcy Court in your county to file for bankruptcy.**

The Voluntary Petition is the first sheet of the Bankruptcy Petition and includes such information as the name and address of the debtor, and the amount and kind of debt that is being eliminated. Like a tax return, schedules accompany the basic petition, based on the type of bankruptcy filing.

Sometimes a local bankruptcy court will have its own rules or schedules which must accompany a bankruptcy filing. It's important to check your local bankruptcy court website before you file. If the filing is incomplete it can be bounced. In fact, a key reason bankruptcy filings are dismissed is that forms are not submitted or properly completed. A good bankruptcy attorney should know the documents needed in your local court.

## Schedule A: Real Estate

This schedule lists all real property that the debtor owns. This may include a home, rental properties, land and/or commercial buildings. Information includes:

- All properties owned solely or jointly, in any state or country.
- Addresses of the properties.
- Values of the properties.

The value of the property is different from the amount of equity an owner has. Equity is the value in the property which the debtor owns. For example, if a property is worth $100,000 but has a $120,000 mortgage on it (because it has declined in value) the owner has no equity in it. In this case, your home is sometimes called **"underwater."** If the property is worth $100,000 and has a $90,000 mortgage on it, the owner has $10,000 of equity.

For a Chapter 7 bankruptcy filing, the owner often has little or no equity in property he or she owns. Certain states enable a filer to protect a substantial amount of equity in a home. The goal is to make sure that the owner's equity can be protected.

# Chapter 7 Bankruptcy Forms

Your bankruptcy petition must include the following schedules and forms, as applicable:

- Voluntary Petition Cover Page
- Declaration Page
- Schedule A: Real Estate
- Schedule B: Personal Property
- Schedule C: Exempt Property
- Schedule D: Secured Creditors
- Schedule E: Priority Debts
- Schedule F: Eliminating Creditors
- Schedule G: Eliminating Leases and Contracts
- Schedule H: Notifying Cosigners of Bankruptcy Filing
- Schedule I: Your Income
- Schedule J: Household Expenses
- Property Exemptions
- Statement of Financial Affairs (SOFA): Property Transfers Prior to Filing
- Paying Attorney Fees: The Compensation Statement
- Statement of Intention: Home and Car Loans
- Creditor Matrix: List of Creditors
- Means Test

## REAL LIFE EXAMPLE

Ella and Boris are married and own a house that is worth $100,000, with a $75,000 mortgage. For bankruptcy filing purposes, this means the house has only a $25,000 value because the mortgage is deducted from the home's value. Both Ella and Boris are filing for Chapter 7 bankruptcy. In their state, they are allowed to keep $30,000 of home equity; this is an exemption for bankruptcy filing purposes.

Between the amount of the loan and the exemption, the full value of the couple's home is protected, leaving them with $5000 more exemption than the house is worth. Thus, Ella and Boris can safely file for Chapter 7 bankruptcy, because there is no equity left unprotected, and there would be nothing for the court to sell or collect on.

But what if the house were worth $150,000? The bankruptcy court could potentially choose to sell the house because it would yield $45,000 (above the amount of the mortgage and exemptions) which could be used to pay off creditors.

- If the house were sold, the trustee would have to give the debtors $30,000, which is the exemption amount.

- If the trustee tries but is unable to sell the house, the debtors will get possession of the house back after the failed attempt.

If you plan to file for bankruptcy and you own a home, it's important to understand what's at stake.

- To assess your property's true value, sales of other comparable homes in your area can be used as proof of the value of your property.

- If property is held in joint names and only one owner is filing a Chapter 7 bankruptcy, only 50% of the value should be attributed to the person in Schedule A.

- If you have a lot of equity in your home, make sure your attorney calculates the value, exemptions and liens to determine whether the property will be sold to pay other creditors.

# Schedule B: Personal Property

Schedule B lists the debtor's personal property. This includes bank accounts, cars, boats, motorcycles, retirement plans, and even time shares. This may also include money coming due in the future that is known to be due, such as an inheritance or litigation proceeds. A trustee can keep a case open for as long as necessary if, for example, there is an open probate proceeding or pending lawsuit.

Sometimes, items on Schedule B are 100% owned by the filer, such as a paid-off car. Since most people do not want to lose their car, a bankruptcy court may agree to what's called a **"buyout."** With a buyout, a debtor can buy back his property from the trustee by paying the court back the difference of the value of the vehicle and the exemption amount, which is the value that can be protected in the bankruptcy.

### REAL LIFE EXAMPLE

Gene lives in Nevada and owns his car worth $20,000. Gene is seeking to discharge $40,000 of unsecured debt. The exemptions in Nevada may cover and protect up to $16,000 worth of the value of the car. Gene can offer to buy out the rest of the vehicle ($4,000) to protect it from being sold. Gene can repay this buyout amount over a six-month period after the bankruptcy is approved.

The trustee will sometimes agree to lower values in a buyout situation because it eliminates his need to find a buyer for the property as the trustee himself cannot bid on the property.

- If property is owned jointly by two individuals, and only one individual is filing bankruptcy, only half of the value of the property should be attributed to the debtor.

## Schedule C: Exempt Property

Even as you are trying to eliminate debts in bankruptcy, some property can be kept or "protected" despite the bankruptcy. These amounts or properties are referred to as **"exemptions."** Exemptions may differ depending on the state in which you are filing. Each state's exemptions are found here: http://www.betterbankruptcy.com/state-bankruptcy-exemptions/.

Schedule C lists the exemptions that exist in the state where the individual is filing. For example, Illinois allows an exemption of $15,000 for real estate property used as a residence. The exemption is available for each person filing so if a married couple is filing in Illinois, and they live in the same home, $30,000 of the real estate property equity can be protected.

*States have the option to set their own exemptions or use the federal exemption guidelines. It's important to know the rules in your state to know how much property can be protected when a bankruptcy is filed.*

Schedule C usually shows the value of the property, along with the exemption amount. An attorney's input is essential to understanding the maximum exemptions available and how to maximize protection of what you own.

# Typical Exemptions

Federal and state exemptions typically protect some portion of the following items from the bankruptcy proceeding. Most states:

- Protect home equity: Illinois protects $15,000 of home equity and Florida protects 100%, with some restrictions.

- Protect a car up to some amount.

- Fully exempt retirement accounts.

## REAL LIFE EXAMPLE

Jenni lives in Illinois and has a trumpet that is valued at $4,000. She qualifies to file for Chapter 7 but she wants to make sure that the trumpet will be fully protected because she cannot bear to lose it. In Illinois, Jenni has a $4,000 **"wildcard exemption,"** which is an exemption that can be used to protect any personal property. As a result, Jennie:

- Can protect the trumpet but she has to make sure that the trumpet is actually worth only $4,000 and not more than that, because if it is worth more, the trumpet may be sold by the bankruptcy trustee.

- Will not be able to protect any other personal property unless she qualifies for another exemption.

## Schedule D: Secured Creditors

Creditors who have liens on your property (listed on Schedules A and B) are listed on Schedule D. The amount of debt you have on property reduces your equity and therefore increases your chances of qualifying for an exemption. The higher the amount of the secured creditor debt, the lower the value or equity in the property in Schedules A and B; and the easier it is for a debtor to file Chapter 7 bankruptcy or to pay less money back in a Chapter 13 bankruptcy.

### REAL LIFE EXAMPLE

Michael has a vehicle that is worth $30,000, listed on Schedule B. He isn't sure if there are enough exemptions to protect the value in his vehicle but then he remembers that he still owes $35,000 to the lender for the car. The lender is listed on Schedule D. Since the loan exceeds the value of the vehicle, there is no need to find an exemption for this vehicle as it has no value to protect. The bankruptcy court would not try to sell it because by the time the loan is paid off, there is no value left.

# Schedule E: Priority Debts

Certain types of debt are not discharged in bankruptcy and these debts, known as **"priority debts"** are reflected on Schedule E. For example, child support and tax debt incurred within the last three years are priority debts, and are non-dischargeable. Other forms of priority debt must be paid first if any property is sold in a bankruptcy filing. Schedule E lists all the priority creditors for the debtor.

If there are child support or maintenance/alimony payments being made, make sure to put the recipient of those payments on Schedule E. Even if there are no back payments, recipients of support payments always have to be listed.

### REAL LIFE EXAMPLE

Thomas is filing for Chapter 7 bankruptcy. He pays child support to his ex-wife. Thomas must list his ex-wife's name and address on Schedule E so that she can receive notice of his bankruptcy filing.

# Schedule F: Eliminating Creditors

Schedule F lists a debtor's unsecured creditors. These creditors may include: credit cards, medical bills, personal loans and miscellaneous bills. The schedule requires you to include the address, account number, type of debt, and the approximate amount owed for each creditor. Here are some of the rules to keep in mind:

- The amount owed is not as important as the name of the creditor and its address.

- For larger companies, any address that they use as a contact address is appropriate to use on this form.

- All creditors should be listed. A debtor cannot choose to keep some credit cards while eliminating others as the court wants to ensure that all creditors of the same type are treated equally.

- If the debtor has paid significant sums to some creditors in the three months prior to filing, the court can recoup funds the creditor that was paid.

- Some debt payments prior to filing may be protected by an exemption.

---

*Generally only creditors notified of the bankruptcy filing can be discharged. It is essential to list all creditors on the Schedule F to make sure they are eliminated when the filing is complete.*

---

If you repay loans to relatives shortly before a bankruptcy filing, they may be subject to recoupment in bankruptcy. Some of this money can be exempted with available exemptions that can be used on anything (such as a wildcard exemption).

Schedule F should include every creditor who is owed money and does not have a security interest in property the debtor owns. This includes friends and relatives and protects the debtor from being later sued by these people in the future. If a relative's or friend's loan is not named on Schedule F as a creditor, that debt will not be discharged.

*A creditor must get notice from the bankruptcy court regarding the bankruptcy filing, to be covered by the discharge. The creditor cannot collect any funds from the debtor, from the time it's notified of the bankruptcy filing, if the debt is dischargeable.*

**REAL LIFE EXAMPLE**

Michelle and Robert file for Chapter 7 bankruptcy. Their creditors include credit card companies such as Life Finance, Orange Credit, and Apple Incorporated. They also owe money to Sonic Credit, which holds a lien on their car. Michelle and Robert should list all the creditors listed above (except Sonic Credit) on Schedule F, because they are unsecured creditors. Sonic Credit is a secured creditor and would be listed on Schedule D.

## Schedule G: Eliminating Leases and Contracts

When you file for bankruptcy, you can also eliminate obligations under leases for personal or business rentals. Although you'll have to vacate the space, you are no longer on the hook for the lease term, or rental fees, which may be a big relief. Leases and contracts that are not yet fully performed (executory contracts) are listed on Schedule G.

Regardless of whether a lease goes on Schedule G, the person collecting on the lease such as the landlord has to be listed on Schedule F as well, or on Schedule D, if a security deposit is held. A security deposit means the landlord is a secured creditor, because it holds property on a debt that does not have to be returned unless the debt is satisfied.

Yelena owns a cupcake business and leases the building which houses her cupcake store. Business has been down and Yelena has decided to close up the shop and file for Chapter 7 bankruptcy, personally, since all the debt in the business is personally guaranteed by Yelena. Upon filing, Yelena's landlord has to be listed on both Schedules G and F to properly file the bankruptcy. The address of the landlord should be listed as well.

# Schedule H: Notifying Cosigners

If a bankruptcy filer has a cosigner on an existing loan at the time of filing, that person is notified via Schedule H. A cosigner may be involved for a car or home loan. A discharge in bankruptcy may leave the cosigner as the sole person liable for the debt. This may mean that they have to pay the debt in full, or suffer their own consequences. In short, a cosigner is generally fully responsible for a debt if the primary debtor files for bankruptcy.

Many times, cosigners are not listed. And yet if they are not listed, they can assert a claim against the debtor in the future, claiming that they relied on the debtor's payments on the items that were cosigned.

Erika buys a car and her sister, Karina, cosigns on the vehicle because Erika's credit isn't good enough to purchase the vehicle on her own. When Erika decides to file for Chapter 7 bankruptcy, she has to list Karina and her address on Schedule H of the bankruptcy filing so that Karina knows that Erika may no longer be liable to pay on the vehicle. This means that Karina may have to keep up the car payments or risk ruining her own credit.

## Schedule I: Your Income

For Chapter 7 bankruptcy, the less income the debtor has, the greater the chance that the filing will go through without issue. The debtor's income is listed on Schedule I.

- If only one person is filing but that individual is married, both incomes have to be listed as the bankruptcy court considers a household income. The filing also requires titles, place of employment and years worked for both spouses.

- If the filer has more than one job, this information and the income should be listed for all jobs.

- Amounts received from Social Security are included as income.

- Direct payroll payments for items such as medical insurance are included.

- Expected income changes, e.g., on account of job loss or salary reduction, are also taken into account on Schedule I.

_____

*For Chapter 7 bankruptcy, you're trying to prove that after you pay your expenses (listed on Schedule J) there is no income left over to pay any creditors. This must be considered as you prepare Schedule I.*

_____

# Schedule J: Household Expenses

Most people who file for Chapter 7 bankruptcy have expenses that exceed their income and this is their sole reason for filing. Schedule J in a bankruptcy filing lists the household expenses of the debtor. This form can also list the debts of the non-filing spouse, if the filer is married. Every expense, including child expenses, health club expenses, etc., should be listed.

There are limits as to how much can be listed on Schedule J so as to not give the Bankruptcy court a reason to dismiss the case. Thus, the expenses on Schedule J have to be reasonable. For example, spending $500 per month on clothes would not be seen as reasonable. However, spending $500 per month on daycare expenses for young children would be a legitimate expense if it can be proved.

# Property Exemptions

Some of what you own is protected in a Chapter 7 bankruptcy filing. Each state may have its own rules as to what can be protected. These amounts are referred to as exemptions. It's essential to know what you can protect, before you file, because once a Chapter 7 bankruptcy is filed, it cannot voluntarily be rescinded. If an obvious mistake was made such as a duplicate case filed for the same person, the court may permit this case to be dismissed but it would be up to the judge's discretion.

Protection in bankruptcy means that the exempt amount or item cannot be touched by the bankruptcy court. For example, if a debtor has $2,000 in the bank and that amount is exempted, this cannot be touched by the bankruptcy court.

Most states exempt retirement accounts completely. However, that only applies if the retirement account is intact. If the debtor takes money out of the account, the money that is taken out is no longer protected and other exemptions have to be used. Thus, it is always wise to rollover retirement accounts by following the specific rollover requirements of the tax laws and retirement account institution.

---

*Exemptions are the main reason debtors should obtain help from a qualified attorney when filing for bankruptcy. Sometimes an exemption seems clear but it is not what it seems. In order to avoid losing property, debtors are encouraged to obtain professional help.*

---

## REAL LIFE EXAMPLE

John is filing for Chapter 7 bankruptcy. He lists all his property on Schedule B which includes a checking account with $10,000. He believes that he can use the federal exemptions and cover the full value of the account. However, he doesn't realize that his state does not allow federal exemptions and he has to use state exemptions that only cover $4,000 in a bank account. Thus, once he files for bankruptcy, he may lose up to $6,000 in the account. A debtor cannot voluntarily rescind his filing, and a lot is at stake if John doesn't know which exemptions apply in his state.

# Transfer Prior to Filing

There are times before a bankruptcy when debtors will sell or give away property. When this happens, depending on the state, these transactions will have to be listed in the filing. The reason this is done is to make sure that debtors don't give away their most valued possessions right before filing in an attempt to safeguard them from their creditors. If the court finds out that this has been done, creditors actually have the right to recover the items from the person that the debtor gave the property to.

The **"Statement of Financial Affairs (SOFA)"** is where these items are disclosed. The list must include items like income the debtor earned in the prior two years. The SOFA also includes information concerning whether the debtor is being sued and by whom. Other miscellaneous information such as the residence of the debtor in the preceding three years is also set forth.

Most of SOFA is usually not filled out. However, such items as recent transfers have to be looked at carefully. Failure to report these transfers can create a really bad situation for the debtor because the court can go after the recipient of the transferred property to recover it.

## REAL LIFE EXAMPLE

Laura sold her vehicle to her mother for $1,000 in May of 2014. The car at the time was worth $5,000. In September 2014, Laura decides to file for Chapter 7 bankruptcy. Laura has to list this transfer in the SOFA or the bankruptcy court may cite Laura for fraud and invalidate her bankruptcy if they find that she has not listed this transfer.

Since Laura sold the car for less than it was worth, she may have to pay the court $4,000 or the court may pursue Laura's mother for the vehicle. Laura may be able to protect the value with exemptions, if they are available.

# Attorney Compensation Statement

Attorneys' fees are set forth on the **"compensation statement."** Usually, nothing should be owed to an attorney at the end because it is difficult for attorneys to collect fees after a bankruptcy filing. Attorneys are also considered creditors and cannot bill the client post-bankruptcy filing for a contract that was made before the bankruptcy. The only exception is if a special agreement is filed.

# Statement of Intention: Home and Car Loans

When filing for bankruptcy, you have the right to eliminate all your loans, including the loans on a car or a house. You cannot keep the house or car if you eliminate the loans but if you are willing to part with the house and car, these loans can be eliminated.

The **"Statement of Intention"** is a notice to creditors about the debtor's wishes concerning keeping home or car loans. This statement informs the creditor and the bankruptcy court whether the debtor plans to keep the items or surrender them to the creditor. This statement does not have a binding effect on the debtor so the debtor can change his mind after it is filed without many consequences.

### REAL LIFE EXAMPLE

Daniel files for Chapter 7 bankruptcy. He has a car with a loan, that he wants to keep. He puts his decision to retain the vehicle on the Statement of Intention but after the bankruptcy concludes, he decides that he can no longer afford to keep the car. He can return the car to the lender without consequence as long as the he has not filed a **"reaffirmation agreement"** during the bankruptcy. If he has not filed a reaffirmation agreement, he will not have to pay the lender anything but must return the vehicle.

# List of Creditors: Creditor Matrix

All of the filer's creditors and their addresses (not only those included in the bankruptcy) must be listed on a main creditor list called the **"creditor matrix."** This list is always used when any amendments are filed and it is attached to notices that accompany bankruptcy motions.

---

*All creditors on the creditor matrix receive notices concerning the bankruptcy filing. They are notified when anything happens in a bankruptcy case.*

---

# Too Much Income:
# So-called "Abuse" Cases

Every person who files for bankruptcy has to fill out a means test to prove that income is below the state filing median and the debtor is qualified to file for bankruptcy. The means test reports income for the six months prior to the bankruptcy filing.

If a filer has suffered a job loss and has high income for part of the period, this could cause income to be above the median. A filing is considered an "abuse" case if the means test shows that the debtor is over the required median income to file a Chapter 7 bankruptcy, and the deductions allowed in the means test don't bring it under the limit.

If this occurs:

- The bankruptcy trustee will expect the filer to file a "Debtor's Rebuttal of a Presumption of Abuse" to tell the court why the debtor should still be allowed to file.

- Often a sufficient explanation is that the debtor's income will be reduced shortly because unemployment income will end.

- A rebuttal has to be filed in order for further investigation not to take place and the future income has to fall under the median with deductions to qualify the individual to file a Chapter 7 bankruptcy.

# Chapter 13 Bankruptcy

A Chapter 13 bankruptcy formulates a repayment plan to pay back creditors anywhere from ten to one hundred percent of the debt owed. The main strategy of a Chapter 13 bankruptcy is to keep the payments as low as possible.

Many of the filing procedures for Chapter 13 are the same as for Chapter 7. For example, Schedules A through F are filed in the same manner, and exemptions are allotted in the same manner as well. Here we'll cover the differences.

A Chapter 13 bankruptcy can last from a few months up to sixty months. A Chapter 7 bankruptcy, on the other hand, is generally completed in a few months. An attorney is often essential for a Chapter 13 filing, because expertise is needed to figure out the financials to keep a debtor's monthly payments as low as possible.

## Chapter 13 Exemptions

The main reason people file a Chapter 13 bankruptcy is because they have too much equity in a car or a house to be able to file under Chapter 7 and yet do not have sufficient means to pay their debts. As a result, the amount of non-exempt property should be kept to a minimum.

---

*Unlike a Chapter 7 filing, a Chapter 13 bankruptcy trustee cannot take property. Instead, if there is more equity in property than allowed, the amount of monthly payments will increase.*

---

### REAL LIFE EXAMPLE

Claire is filing for Chapter 13 bankruptcy. She doesn't make a lot of money but she does have some money left over every month, and she has about $20,000 of credit card debt. Claire owns a piano that is worth $10,000. In the state where Claire lives, there is only a $4,000 exemption for personal property.

Claire doesn't want to lose her piano so she files for Chapter 13 bankruptcy. Claire can keep her piano, but will have to pay back $6,000 in debt ($10,000 piano value, less $4,000 exemption) to reflect the overage in her exempt property that she retains. In short, Claire will have to pay back at least $6,000 of her $20,000 credit card debt.

# The Automatic Stay

The automatic stay protection from creditors in a Chapter 13 may last for as long as it takes to pay off debt on the repayment plan for up to sixty months. During this time, a Chapter 13 bankruptcy will protect a home from being sold or a car from being repossessed. As long as Chapter 13 payments and monthly mortgage payments are paid on time, the automatic stay is in effect unless a creditor files a motion to remove this protection.

If payments are missed and the case is then dismissed, the automatic stay will be removed when the case is dismissed. The net effect is that the debtor will be in the same position as if the bankruptcy had never been filed.

## REAL LIFE EXAMPLE

Gerry files for bankruptcy to protect his house. He's behind on mortgage payments. The missed payment amount will be part of the bankruptcy repayment plan. From the time of filing, Gerry will make the required plan payments every month, in addition to the regular mortgage payment. If either of those two payments are missed consecutively and not made up, the automatic stay that protects the house form being put into foreclosure by the mortgage company can be lifted and thus eliminated.

# Protecting Cosigners in a Chapter 13 Bankruptcy

Cosigners of the person filing for items such as a car or house are protected in a Chapter 13 bankruptcy even if: (1) they have not themselves filed, as long as the bankruptcy is not dismissed and (2) as long as the creditor does not ask for the protection for a particular item to be removed.

# Calculating the Chapter 13 Repayment Plan

The Chapter 13 Plan is calculated based on two different criteria: the "income-based plan" and the "equity-based plan."

## Income-based Plan

The income-based plan calculates the repayment amount based on the amount that the debtor is over on the means test based on their state's median. These medians can be found here: http://www.justice.gov/ust/eo/bapcpa/meanstesting.htm

The means test itself is somewhat complicated. If the debtor's has excess disposable income under the means test, payments in that amount will have to be made toward unsecured debt over a sixty month period.

### REAL LIFE EXAMPLE

Elsa has $24,000 of unsecured debt and excess disposable income of $200 per month on the means test. As a result, Elsa will have to pay back $12,000 ($200/month x 60 months) of her unsecured debt. This would be a 50% plan.

If Elsa's debt is only $10,000, she would have to pay it back in full if her disposable income is $200/month and this would be a 100% plan.

## Equity-based Plan

The equity-based plan is calculated based on the amount of equity that the debtor has in property that cannot be fully protected by exemptions.

### REAL LIFE EXAMPLE

Henry owns a house worth $100,000, with a $50,000 loan on it and protected by $15,000 in exemptions. Henry would have to pay back an estimated $35,000 in debt so the property is not at risk for being sold.

Several factors are taken into account to formulate a repayment plan:

- If debtors pass the means test or are under the state median amount, they can do a thirty-six-month plan, but most debtors opt to do a sixty-month plan, to keep monthly payments low. The debt amount is divided over sixty months instead of thirty-six months.

- If debtors do not pass the means test, repayments are over sixty months unless they have a 100% plan, in which case they can opt to pay off all their debt earlier.

- If the plan is based on value of equity (instead of income) repayment terms will include interest payments.

- The type of debt being repaid matters. For example, for taxes due or mortgage payments, the full default must be paid back within the sixty-month period. A debtor must make current and default payments during this period.

- For student loans, it is possible to pay 10% on the student loans for five years, as well as make payments on other debt, under a 10% plan. However, student loans are not dischargeable in bankruptcy and the rest due will be due after the bankruptcy is over.

*Most Chapter 13 repayment plans are not based on equity ownership. This gives debtors five years to repay, with zero interest, as opposed to paying high interest rates on credit card debt.*

Another advantage to a Chapter 13 bankruptcy is that debtors can put a car into a Chapter 13 bankruptcy repayment plan and pay it off in a five-year period with a much lower interest rate (usually prime plus about 1.5%) than their current rate. As a result, bankruptcy can help a person catch up on payments. In this case, the debtor would be paying the full amount of the car off in the bankruptcy, and he or she would not be making any additional payments.

## Reduced Car Loan Payments: Cram Down

When debtors file for Chapter 13 bankruptcy, they can potentially decrease their monthly car payments as well as their interest rate. This lets the debtor pay back only the amount that a vehicle is worth if it still has a lien on it, rather than the whole value of the original car loan. This is known as a **"cram down."** To qualify, the vehicle has to be for personal use and the loan must have been taken out more than 910 days (2.5 years) before the Chapter 13 bankruptcy was filed.

Here's how a cram down works:

- The filing will use the lowest possible value of the car to leave room to negotiate with the lender as to how much the car is actually worth.

- Once the value is agreed upon, the interest rate for the secured loan goes down to prime plus about 1.5 points and the value is then paid back in full in the plan.

- The amount of the loan in excess of the actual current value of the car (the unsecured portion) is paid back at the same percent as the rest of the unsecured creditors in the plan.

---

*With a cram down, the debtor pays back less than the actual loan at more favorable interest rates. He agrees to pay off an unsecured loan, but does not pay the value in excess of the car's actual current value.*

---

## Creditor Payments and Objections

In a Chapter 13 bankruptcy, the creditors holding car loans and mortgages have to be paid enough every month to offset the monthly depreciation of the asset. The goal is for the creditor to be compensated for secured property each month. If the creditor is not protected and the property depreciates, it is likely the creditor will object to the plan.

It is very typical to have some objections to the plan filed in a Chapter 13 case. These objections usually center on the actual amounts of the loan values or arrears being listed to be repaid back in the plan.

For example, if a debtor thinks he's behind $12,000 in his mortgage payments but the actual amount is really $15,000, the mortgage company will file an objection to make sure that they are repaid what they are actually owed in the plan.

Objections should be expected and creditors are wrong sometimes. It is important to be able to amend the plan to take into account the objection in order to resolve the objection so that the plan can be approved by the court.

## Making Payments Under Chapter 13

Chapter 13 payments are made to the trustee every month for the duration of the repayment plan. These payments can normally be made in only two ways:

1. A debtor can send the payment to the trustee via a certified check or a money order to a PO box address.

2. The debtor can have the payments taken out of a paycheck. Recently, many trustees have started using a bank draft option as well.

## Chapter 13 Required Hearing and Documentation

A 341 hearing is held in a Chapter 13 bankruptcy to make sure the paperwork is filed correctly and the debtor has correctly stated his/her income. The court wants to be certain that the debtor can pay under a repayment plan.

Usually, a few amendments will be made after the hearing. The debtor should wait for all objections to come in, before the petition is amended. A petition can be amended to accommodate objections.

## Missed Payments

If more than one but usually at least two payments have been missed in a Chapter 13 plan, the plan can be dismissed if the trustee files a motion to dismiss. If this happens and the debtor has funds to get current, the trustee can withdraw the motion. If the debtor does not have the funds to cure the default, the case will be dismissed.

## Confirmation Hearing to Approve the Plan

For a debtor to receive a discharge in a Chapter 13 bankruptcy, the judge must approve the plan in a confirmation hearing. If the debtor is making payments on time, all objections are resolved, and all requested amendments are made, plans are usually confirmed.

If a plan is not feasible, meaning that the income the debtor receives is not sufficient to make payments into the plan, the plan won't be approved. For example, if a debtor has no income and the plan calls him to make payments of $200 a month, then the plan will not be confirmed and confirmation will be denied. Eventually, the case will be dismissed.

# Paying Creditor Claims

Creditors must file claims to be paid within ninety days after the 341 hearing, in a Chapter 13 bankruptcy. If a claim is not made by this so called **"bar date,"** the claim will be barred and the creditor will not get paid through the plan. Instead they will have to wait until after the bankruptcy is discharged if the debt is an unsecured dischargeable debt.

If a creditor is not listed in a Chapter 13 Schedule F, and the case is discharged, the creditor can still ask to be paid because they had no chance of making a claim in the bankruptcy and filing a claim by the bar date.

Many smaller creditors may not make claims. However, this does not mean that the debtor will pay less than what the repayment was calculated to be unless the plan requires repayment of every debt owed. Instead, if there is less than a 100% repayment plan, creditors that did make a claim will get paid more of their claim than the percentage they were first given as a payout.

If creditors are not notified in the original filing, they should be notified by making an amendment to the filing or by faxed notice. The debtor should make sure to keep the fax receipt as proof that the creditor knew of the filing before the bar date expires for the creditor to make a claim.

# Chapter 13 Bankruptcy Trustees

The trustee in a Chapter 13 bankruptcy must make sure the repayment plan serves all creditors equally and fairly. The trustee can object to a plan if he or she determines it does not treat creditors fairly. The trustee can also object to the feasibility of the plan if he or she believes the debtor won't be able to make payments for the full duration of the plan.

## Debtor Options and Requests

Motions can be filed as part of a Chapter 13 proceeding for a variety of reasons. For example, a motion can be filed to modify the plan to eliminate second mortgages if the value of the first mortgage exceeds the current value of the home. Motions are important and can have a huge impact on the case. This is why attorneys are usually compensated for the whole duration of the plan upon hiring and are paid every month with all the other creditors every time a debtor makes a payment (at a 100% rate, just like secured creditors regardless of how much the unsecured creditors are paid).

## Credit Counseling

As with a Chapter 7 bankruptcy, Chapter 13 filers have to complete a credit counseling class before filing for bankruptcy and proof of completion has to be filed with the court. After a bankruptcy petition is filed, the debtor has to complete a debtor education class, with certificate proof filed to receive a discharge at the end of the plan.

---

*Because of the length of a repayment plan, debtors often forget they have to complete the debtor education class. If they do, the case will be dismissed and an additional fee must be paid to reopen the case and file the certificate. It is advisable to take the debtor education class soon after the filing to avoid this trap.*

---

## Domestic Support Obligation Disclosure

A **"Domestic Support Obligation Disclosure"** has to be filed with the court after a Chapter 13 bankruptcy is filed and before a discharge is given in a Chapter 13 bankruptcy. This form discloses whether the debtor has any domestic support obligations, whether those obligations are timely, and the current employment status of the debtor. Usually it is sent to the debtor in the beginning and before the completion of the plan.

## Eliminating Debt in a Chapter 13 Bankruptcy

Once debtors are given a bankruptcy discharge, they are discharged from all dischargeable debt, regardless of how much money they paid to unsecured creditors. This only occurs if the debtors complete all plan payments and all creditors were notified.

This means that no creditors that are owed money by the debtor prior to filing bankruptcy can collect on this money post-bankruptcy unless the debt is a non-dischargeable debt or unless the creditor was not given notice of the filing.

---

*If a debtor's case is dismissed and not discharged due to missed plan payments, then the creditor can still attempt to collect on the debt owed by the debtor.*

---

# Special Circumstances

Certain elements in a bankruptcy proceeding get special treatment. These include divorce decrees, student loans, and business obligations.

## Divorce Decrees

Divorce decrees always trump bankruptcies, and if something is written into a divorce decree as far as obligation on debt, the bankruptcy is subject to it. For example, if a divorce decree says that Spouse A has to be pay off the credit card that Spouse A and Spouse B had together jointly, Spouse A cannot file bankruptcy to discharge the debt.

Here's why: If Spouse A files for bankruptcy, the credit card company will sue Spouse B for non-payment if no payments are being made. Then, Spouse B can sue Spouse A for violating the divorce decree court order and Spouse B will win. However, if both Spouse A and B file for bankruptcy, and the debt is dischargeable, this issue can be overcome.

## Businesses

An involuntary bankruptcy can be filed by a creditor to force the debtor to go into bankruptcy and to have the trustee allocate the assets to the creditors. This can only be done if debtors have a business in their name primarily for business debt. This is done very infrequently.

If business loans are not being repaid because the business is not making any money, an individual may choose to file a personal Chapter 7 bankruptcy in order to get rid of the personal liability on the loans. Frequently, small business owners take loans in the name of the business that they personally guaranty. Personally guaranteed loans are part of the bankruptcy.

The business will still have liability on these loans but as most small business have few or no assets, the business can close and all liability will be eliminated for the debtor after the personal bankruptcy.

## Student Loan Discharge

It is possible to discharge student loans in both a Chapter 7 and Chapter 13 bankruptcy, but it is very difficult. In short, debtors must prove that they will never be able to make enough income in their future other than to provide them with the necessities they need to live. This is a tough thing to prove. Typically only disabled debtors who will be unable to work for their entire life can meet this level of proof.

# Alternatives to Bankruptcy

**There are some alternatives to bankruptcy depending on the type and amount of debt incurred.**

The alternatives to bankruptcy may not be viable for most people. Here are some ways to approach things:

- An individual may receive an inheritance or win the lottery, thus creating an opportunity to pay back debt.

- Credit card companies often will negotiate debt rather than receive little or no payment as an unsecured creditor in a bankruptcy.

- Mortgage holders may agree to loan modifications or consolidations to at least recoup some of their investment if they determine the borrower is at risk or the home is worth less than the mortgage.

Be wary of credit consolidation companies that promise something that sounds too good to be true. It is likely that it is too good to be true, and instead their fees will add to your debt.

# Life After Bankruptcy

**Once a bankruptcy is over, individuals who have filed must follow a few tips in order to rebuild their credit.**

Due to the economy, many individuals are filing bankruptcies and it has become easier for people to obtain future credit and to rebuild their credit. Here are some rules of the road to keep yourself on track:

- It's essential to keep current on all payments regarding any reaffirmed debt.

- Rebuild credit by getting a secured credit card, which is really a debit card but counts as a credit card for credit reporting purposes.

- Consider applying for a high interest card, which you pay off timely, to rebuild your credit. If you don't pay timely, you will incur high interest rates.

- Once your credit improves, you can receive lower interest rates on future credit cards.

# Glossary

**341 hearing:** Mandatory hearing concern income levels that is required for any debtor filing for either Chapter 7 or Chapter 13 Bankruptcy.

**521 documents:** These documents include sixty days' worth of proof of income, for the sixty days prior to filing. This typically includes pay stubs and the prior year's tax return, or return last filed. In a Chapter 13 bankruptcy, this includes four years' of prior tax returns.

**Asset case:** A Chapter 7 bankruptcy that includes more property than can be protected.

**Automatic stay:** Period after a bankruptcy is filed during which notified creditors cannot try to collect on any debts or pursue new garnishments.

**Bar date:** A deadline established ninety days after a 341 hearing by which creditors must file claims.

**Buyout:** Part of a bankruptcy which enables a debtor to buy back property from the trustee for the difference between its value and the exemption amount, or some other negotiated amount.

**Compensation Statement:** Reflects amount of attorney fees in a Chapter 13 bankruptcy filing.

**Cosigners:** In the context of a bankruptcy, those who contractually agree to make payments when the debtor cannot.

**Cram down:** Part of a repayment plan which essentially refinances an existing debt during the repayment plan period for low or no interest, based on the current value of the asset.

**Credit Counseling Certificate:** Document which must be filed with the court to prove the debtor attended the required credit counseling or debt education classes.

**Creditor matrix:** Form filed with the bankruptcy petition which indicates all of the debtor's creditors and their addresses.

**Debtor:** In the context of a bankruptcy, a debtor is the person or business that files for bankruptcy.

**Debtor education class:** Required class a debtor must attend and obtain a certificate of completion for, to qualify for a bankruptcy discharge.

**Discharge:** This term signifies the elimination of debt through bankruptcy.

**Domestic Support Obligation Disclosure:** A form disclosing whether the debtor has any domestic support obligations, whether those obligations are timely, and the current employment status of the debtor.

**Exemptions:** In the context of a bankruptcy, this refers to specific property and/or value limits for property that may be retained by a debtor and unavailable to creditors according to federal or state law. The amount varies depending on where the debtor files.

**Forma Pauperis Motion:** A motion to waive filing fees for bankruptcy court because the debtor is living below the poverty level.

**Garnishment:** When creditors receive payments directly from a paycheck or bank account because they have a court order or consent from the debtor to do so.

# Glossary

**Lien:** Liens are security for the repayment of a debt. A judgment lien secures property owed to a creditor after a successful court proceeding against the debtor. Liens are also placed against property through a mortgage (on real estate) or loan terms (e.g., car loan).

**Means test:** Calculation required to be submitted to bankruptcy court to prove that a filer's income limits qualify for bankruptcy filing.

**Median income:** In the context of a bankruptcy, this refers to a state's threshold value in determining eligibility for bankruptcy filings in that state.

**Notice of Filing:** Form which must accompany filings in bankruptcy court to alert all interested parties about filings in the connection with a case.

**Objection:** Motion filed to disagree with a court filing or request.

**Priority debts:** Debts that cannot be eliminated in bankruptcy and must be paid first. In a Chapter 7 bankruptcy, this includes child support and recent tax debt. It is reported on a Schedule E during the bankruptcy filing.

**Reaffirmation agreement:** An agreement between the creditor and the debtor that reinstates the debt of a debtor after the bankruptcy is discharged. The obligation to pay on this debt survives the bankruptcy.

**Secured debt:** Debt secured by a lien against the property to which it relates. This type of debt is generally not eliminated in bankruptcy unless the individual is also willing to surrender the property (such as a car or home) which is connected to the lien.

**Statement of Financial Affairs (SOFA):** A schedule in the bankruptcy petition that includes information regarding the debtor's past financial information that may not be included in any of the other schedules such as past transfers and past income.

**Statement of Intention:** Schedule filed with the Chapter 7 bankruptcy petition which states the debtor's intention to either keep or surrender property on which there is a lien attached.

**Underwater:** A home in which the unpaid mortgage amount is higher than the current value of the home.

**Unsecured debt:** In the context of a bankruptcy, this type of debt can be fully discharged. It includes credit card debt, leases, personal loans not attached to any property or payday loans, and other types of contract debt. Some types of property, such as furniture, electronics, and jewelry that are secured by "unsecured debt" must be returned to the creditor as part of a bankruptcy.

**Wildcard exemption:** In many states, this is the name of the exemption that can be applied to any personal property.

# About the Author

## Marina Ricci, J.D.

Marina Ricci focuses on bankruptcy and real estate law in Illinois. In addition to being a practicing attorney, Ms. Ricci teaches bankruptcy and real estate law at Harper College in Palatine, Illinois. She especially enjoys writing and counseling clients.

Ms. Ricci received her Bachelors in Business Administration (in finance and international business) from Loyola University Chicago and her law degree from Valparaiso University School of Law. She is licensed to practice law in Illinois.

# About Real Life Legal™

Parker Press Inc., the publisher of Real Life Legal™ creates plain language consumer information on legal, tax, business and financial subjects. Taking aim at info overload and legalese, Parker Press Inc. launched Real Life Legal™ in 2014. Real Life Legal™ provides practical advice, written by lawyers, to help people understand how the law works. Our goal is to provide solid, easy-to-understand information so *you* can decide whether it makes sense to hire a lawyer. Real Life Legal™ wants you to be prepared.

## Available Titles

**Bankruptcy Basics: Chapter 7 and Chapter 13**
Marina Ricci, Esq.

**Business Owners Startup Guide**
Susan G. Parker, Esq. and Lynne Williams, Esq.

**Elder Law: Legal Planning for Seniors**
Susan G. Parker, Esq. and Maria B. Whealan, Esq.

**Employee's Guide to Discrimination and Termination**
Joanne Dekker, Esq.

**Estate Planning: A Road Map for Beginners**
Susan G. Parker, Esq. and Maria B. Whealan, Esq.

**Filing a Homeowner's Claim: Natural Disaster or Not**
Dawn Snyder, Esq.

**A Lawyer's Guide to Home Renovations**
John A. Goodman, Esq.

# Available Titles (Continued)

**Planning for Pets: Trusts, Leash Laws and More**
Joanne Dekker, Esq.

**Planning for Your Special Needs Child**
Amy Newman, Esq.

**Special Needs Education: Navigating for Your Child**
Lynne Williams, Esq.

**Tenant's Guide to Residential Leases**
Nicole Lichtman, Esq.

**U.S. Veterans: Your Rights and Benefits**
Maria B. Whealan, Esq.
with Paul M. Goodson, Esq.

**What to Do When Someone Dies**
Susan G. Parker, Esq.

**You've Been Arrested: Now What?**
Maryam Jahedi, Esq.

# Notes

# Notes

# Notes

# Notes

# Notes

# Notes

# Notes

# Notes

# Notes

# Notes

# Notes

# Notes

# Notes